I WANT TO BE A
PARAMEDIC

Written by
Jocelyn Chua

Edited by
Jonathan Reule

Illustration
Caballero Peza Mauricio
&
Caballero Peza Gabriel Fernando

Storyboard
Keziah Gan

Copyright © 2023 by Unibino Pte. Ltd.

First paperback edition August 2023
ISBN 978-981-17359-0-5

Published by Unibino Pte. Ltd.
31 Rochester Drive Level 3, #03-47 Singapore 138637

www.unibino.com

Can you recall a time when you helped a friend who fell down and hurt themselves? Were you calm, quick, and focused on getting them the help they needed? And would you consider yourself a brave person, unfazed by the sight of blood, needles, cuts, and bruises? If you answered yes to any of these, then the role of a paramedic may be just for you!

A paramedic is a healthcare professional who provides emergency medical relief to patients outside a hospital setting. Paramedics are often the first responders to crisis situations such as road accidents, natural disasters, or other health emergencies. They save lives by stabilising the condition of their patients and transporting them to the nearest hospital for further treatment.

It has been said that a healed human bone was the first sign of civilisation because someone cared enough to stay with the injured person or bring them to safety and then nurse them back to health. While animals that were injured usually died from their wounds in the wild, our human ancestors who had the appropriate tools and support could successfully recover from their injuries.

Empathy and attentiveness are certainly the hallmarks of any healthcare profession, as are the knowledge and tools needed to carry out palliative work on the sick and injured. In ancient times, it was common to use charms and talismans to cure illnesses, as people believed deities and otherworldly forces had the power to heal them. Some cultures had shamans or medicine men and women who carried out healing rituals too.

Many of our predecessors also used plant medicine and natural remedies to treat those who were unwell. They likewise understood the importance of a healthy diet and paid attention to their nutrition as a way of preventing illness. Did you know the Egyptians even had medical specialists who addressed ailments related to different aspects of the body? This could be due to their detailed knowledge of human anatomy from the practice of mummifying their dead!

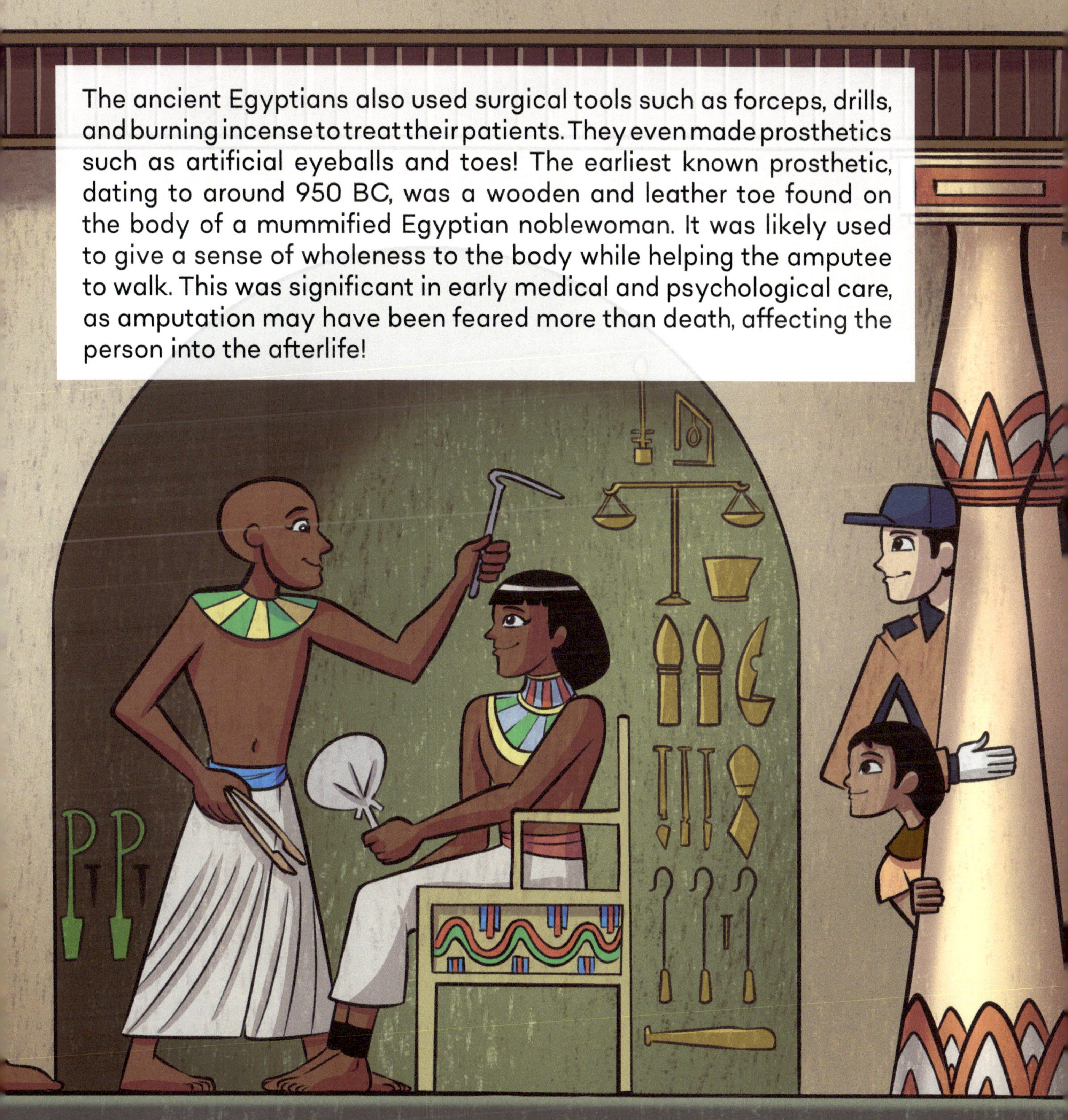
The ancient Egyptians also used surgical tools such as forceps, drills, and burning incense to treat their patients. They even made prosthetics such as artificial eyeballs and toes! The earliest known prosthetic, dating to around 950 BC, was a wooden and leather toe found on the body of a mummified Egyptian noblewoman. It was likely used to give a sense of wholeness to the body while helping the amputee to walk. This was significant in early medical and psychological care, as amputation may have been feared more than death, affecting the person into the afterlife!

Surgery was also used in ancient China. Legend has it that Hua Tuo, the most famous Chinese physician of antiquity, once did an emergency operation on a general shot by a poison arrow. Acting swiftly to prevent the poison from spreading, Hua Tuo cut open the general's wounded arm and proceeded to scrape the poison out of the bone!

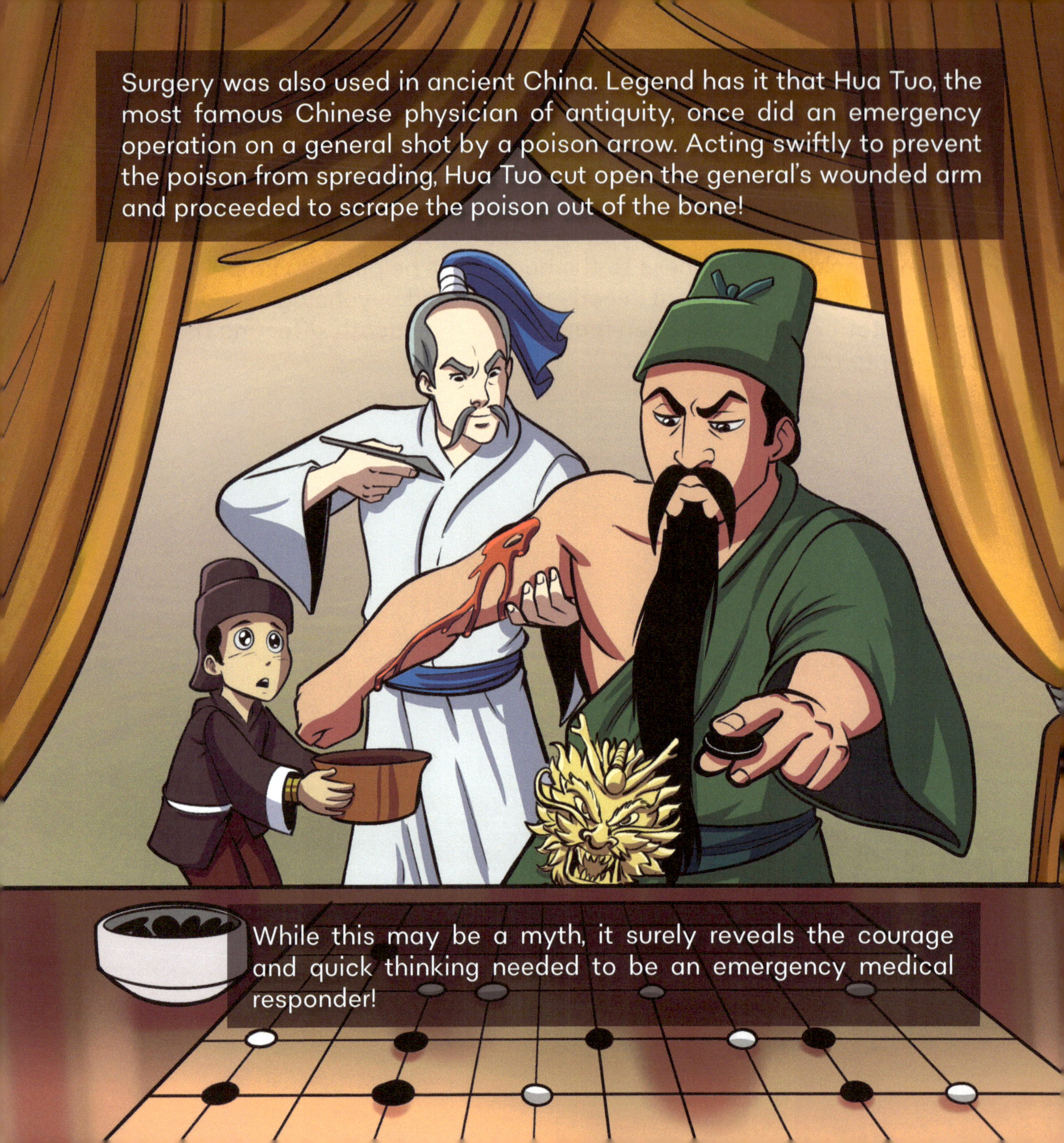

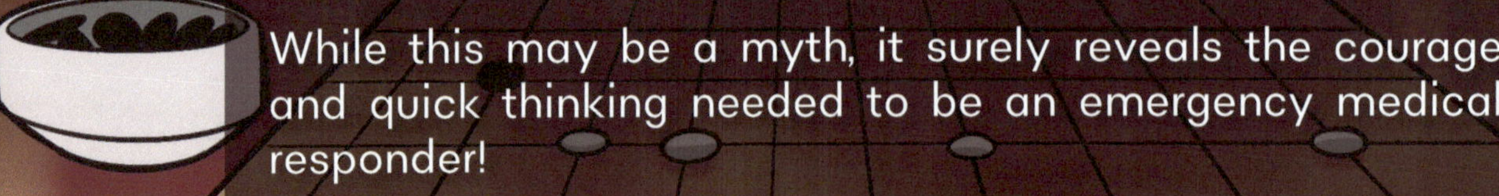

While this may be a myth, it surely reveals the courage and quick thinking needed to be an emergency medical responder!

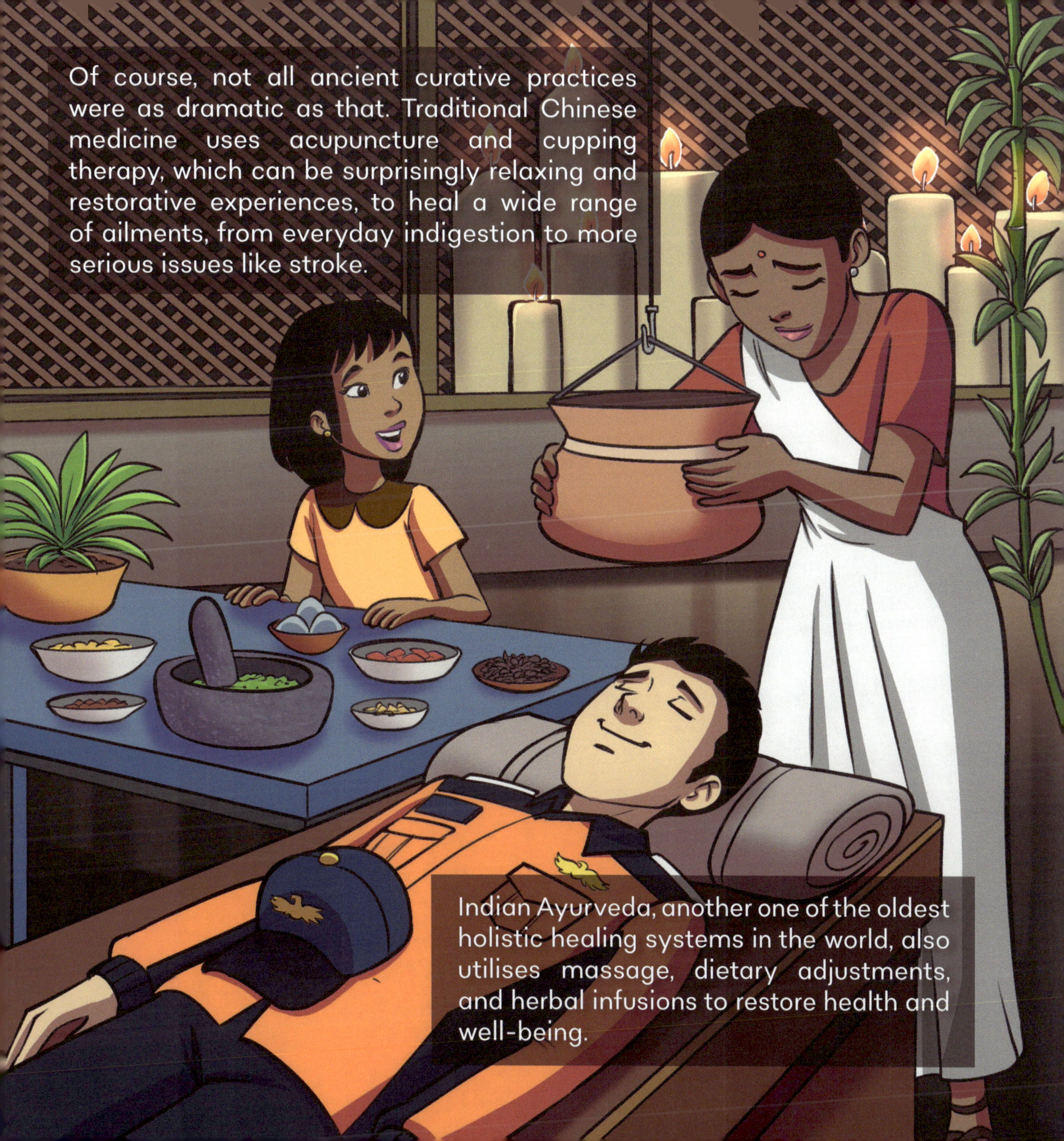

Of course, not all ancient curative practices were as dramatic as that. Traditional Chinese medicine uses acupuncture and cupping therapy, which can be surprisingly relaxing and restorative experiences, to heal a wide range of ailments, from everyday indigestion to more serious issues like stroke.

Indian Ayurveda, another one of the oldest holistic healing systems in the world, also utilises massage, dietary adjustments, and herbal infusions to restore health and well-being.

So before hospitals became commonplace institutions in our world, our ancestors used a variety of medical practices and technology in their time to treat their patients. And besides medical prowess, speed is also essential when it comes to saving lives!

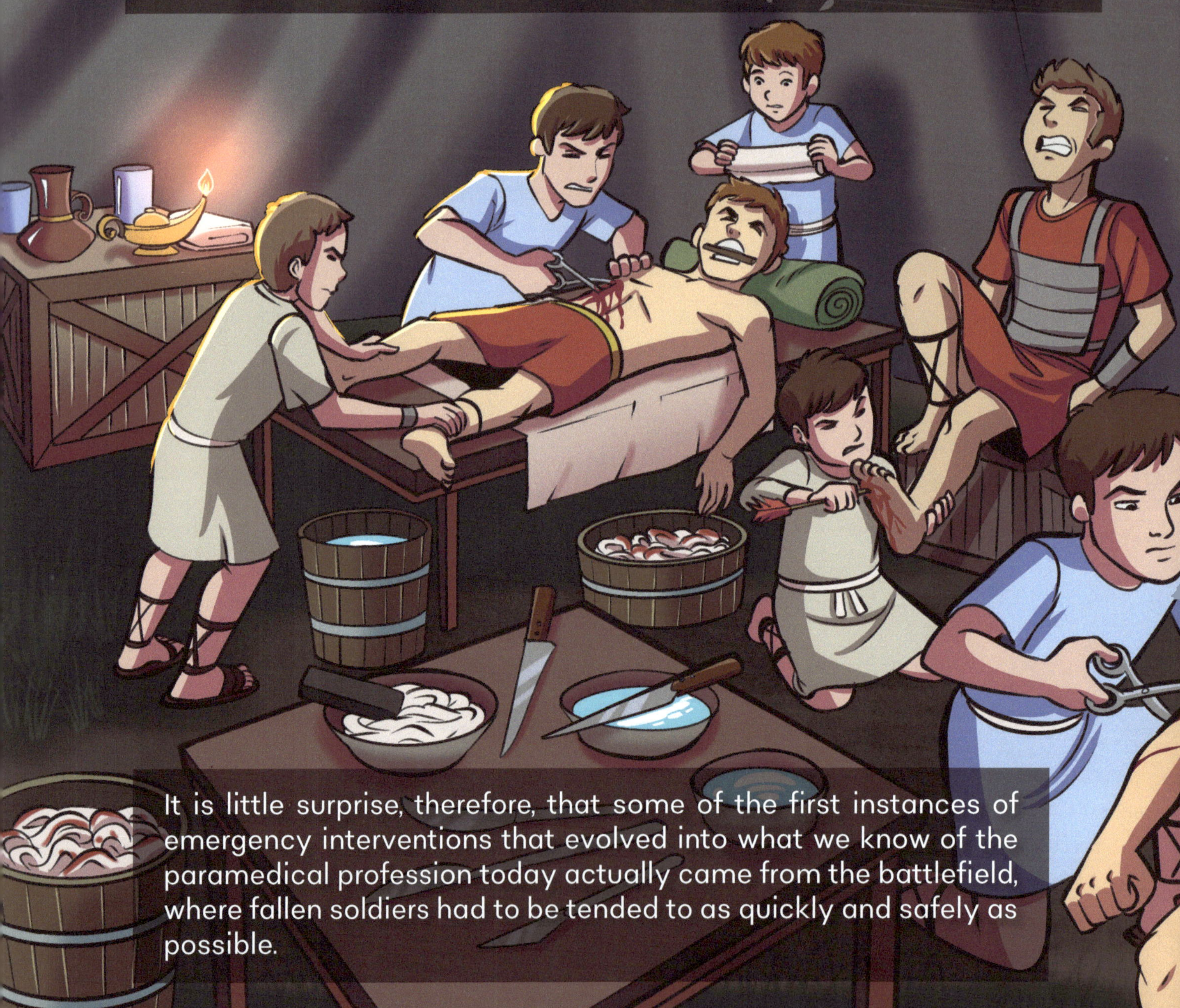

It is little surprise, therefore, that some of the first instances of emergency interventions that evolved into what we know of the paramedical profession today actually came from the battlefield, where fallen soldiers had to be tended to as quickly and safely as possible.

The Romans, for example, had medical corpsmen and practised frontline treatment with soldiers helping to treat one another. They also had a system of casualty collection to efficiently evacuate wounded soldiers along very well-supported logistical lines. Some of the most sophisticated traumatic wound treatments and clean sanitation practices also came from early Roman armies. One could say the Roman military had some of the first and most organised paramedical processes in the world!

With the invention and increasingly widespread use of firearms during warfare over the centuries, medical care also began to evolve and advance to address gunshot wounds and other traumatic injuries on the battlefield. The Napoleonic Wars of the early 1800s was a key historical event that revolutionised and influenced some of the professional paramedical practices that exist in our world today.

Pierre Francois Percy, surgeon to the French Imperial Army commanded by Napoleon Bonaparte, has been credited to have formed the first group of paramedical attendants, known as brancardiers (or 'stretcher-bearers'), dedicated entirely to the care of the wounded on the field.
These wartime medical personnel used collapsible stretchers to transport the battle wounded and wore large hats that stored basic medical supplies like dressings that could be easily brought to fallen soldiers.

Prior to Percy's innovations, many of the battle wounded were either left on the field for dead or removed by their comrades using farm carts - a very bumpy and painful means of transportation indeed! The injured also often waited for days before quite crude surgical treatment was applied, usually consisting of amputation or the agonising poking of wounds to try to locate and extract a musket ball or pieces of shrapnel. Percy's efforts paved the way for more efficient and humane means of medical rescue.

The French also came up with the concept of triage during this time, an official system of prioritising the treatment of wounds based on their severity. It was Napoleon's chief surgeon, Dominique Jean Larrey, who formalised this system so that military casualties were treated based on the level of threat to their lives and not on their rank in the army.

This was a revolutionary shift in humanity's thinking towards medical care. While we can perhaps agree that all human life is worth saving, here was an actual system practising just that!

And did you know that Jean Larrey also invented what is called the flying ambulance? The first of its kind, this was a light two-wheeled horse-drawn wagon that could swiftly and quite comfortably transport wounded soldiers on the still active battlefield! Complete with ventilation, cushions, and an inbuilt spring, the flying ambulance was so named as Larrey adapted it from the design of the agile French artillery carriages (known as artillerie volante or "flying artillery") that could travel nimbly over uneven ground.

Ambulances are indeed an integral part of paramedicine. One crucial development came about during the mid to late 1800s when ambulances were used to actively treat patients on the way to a hospital.

This is significant because instead of merely focusing on transporting the injured to a nearby facility, ambulances became increasingly equipped with the tools to immediately stabilise a patient's condition. Ambulances dispatched from the Bellevue Hospital back in 19th century New York City, for example, were stocked with medical implements such as splints, stomach pumps, and painkillers like morphine.

N°5

Moving into the 1900s, paramedical work continued to evolve from transporting people to equipping frontline responders with more advanced life-saving skills. This opened up the myriad possibilities and types of training for the professional paramedic. One of the earliest instances of a formal paramedic programme was in the United States in 1969, where firefighters were trained to provide advanced life support care, such as administering emergency medications and performing resuscitation procedures on casualties onsite.

From the 1980s to the early 2000s, other forms of ambulances and paramedical support also became increasingly recognised around the world. Have you heard of cycle responders? These are fully trained frontline paramedics who ride bicycles loaded with emergency care devices. They operate in areas that are harder to reach by car or ambulance and are similar to motorcycle paramedics. These speedy two-wheel responders are like human first-aid kits on the move!

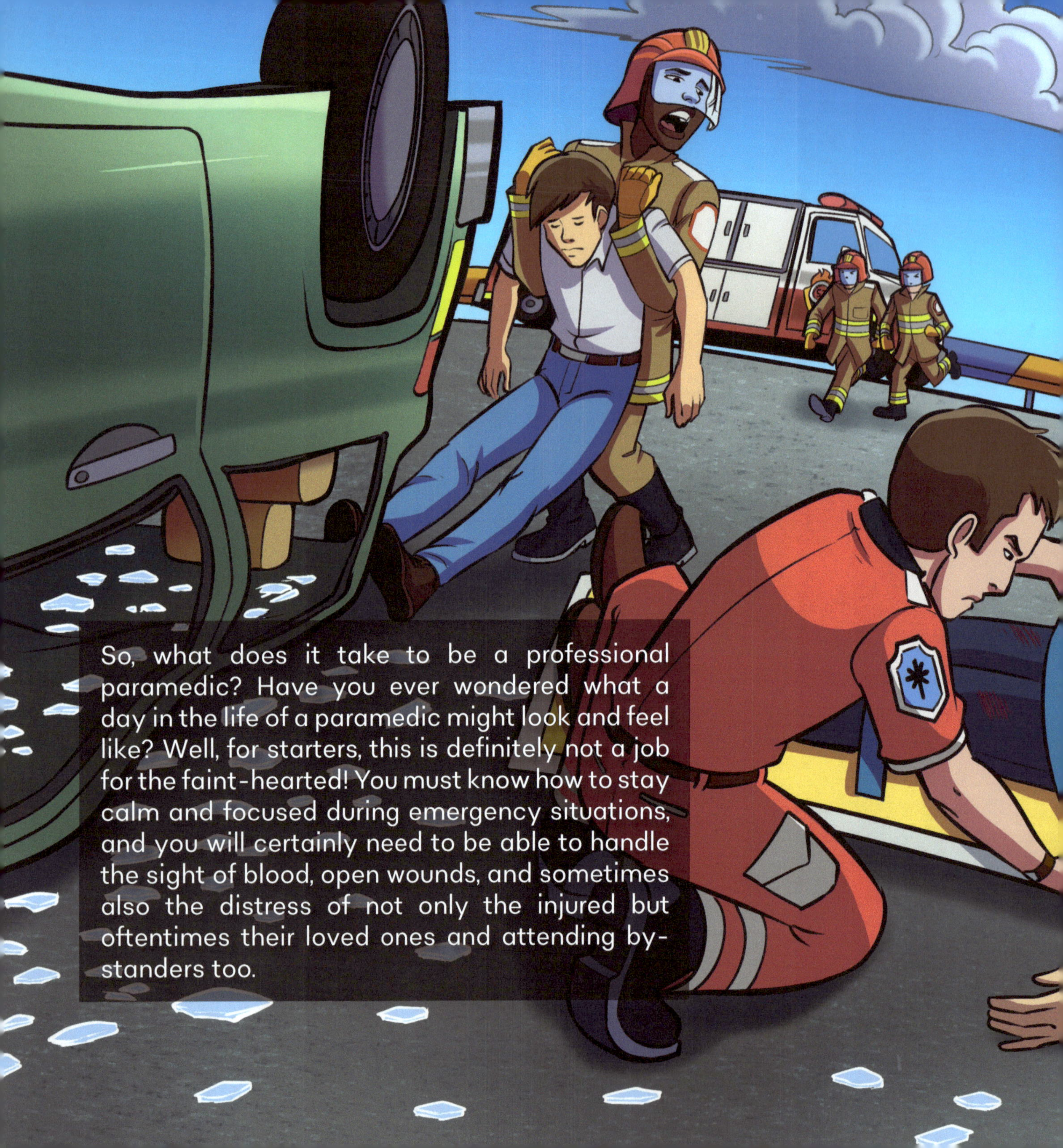

So, what does it take to be a professional paramedic? Have you ever wondered what a day in the life of a paramedic might look and feel like? Well, for starters, this is definitely not a job for the faint-hearted! You must know how to stay calm and focused during emergency situations, and you will certainly need to be able to handle the sight of blood, open wounds, and sometimes also the distress of not only the injured but oftentimes their loved ones and attending by-standers too.

So it is definitely a requirement to be emotionally and mentally resilient as a paramedic, for you never know when an emergency may strike or how intense a situation may get. It also helps to be physically fit in order to perform your duties effectively, such as lifting patients onto stretchers, carrying equipment like oxygen resuscitators, or skilfully navigate physically challenging spaces. Just imagine what it takes to carefully extricate injured civilians stuck inside a car wreckage along a busy road intersection!

Being a paramedic also means knowing how to assess a medical emergency in order to render the most effective life-saving solution. This requires alertness and strong decision-making skills. For example, if you saw someone lying unconscious on the ground, what would be the first thing to do?

Wake them up by shaking their bodies (and risk exacerbating any broken limbs!) or by administering a sharp smell (and risk triggering a seizure!)? The person may have collapsed due to any number of reasons, and it is the task of the paramedic to be able to administer the correct rescue procedures.

And perhaps, above all else, compassion together with a readiness to put oneself oftentimes in harm's way in order to save lives are also timeless tenets that underpin the work of a paramedic.

A stunning example was US Army medic Desmond Doss who, due to his personal and religious beliefs, never carried a firearm during his service in World War II but once managed to single-handedly extract about 75 wounded soldiers left on a battlefield near the edge of a cliff, by lowering them to safety one by one with a self-made pulley. He did it over a span of 12 hours while still under heavy mortar and gunfire!

As you can tell by now, it is no mean feat to be a paramedic, and you will require specialised, and often quite advanced, training to fulfil the specific role that you take on in this field, as there are many different types of paramedics around.

Critical care paramedics fight to save lives en route to a hospital, while general care paramedics tend to support a patient in their own homes. There are also on-location paramedics trained to handle emergencies at large events such as festivals or parades and flight or shipboard paramedics trained to work in aircraft or ship settings.

One way to begin your professional training in paramedicine is to enrol in a state-approved paramedic training programme that includes a mix of classroom lessons and hands-on clinical experience.
This can take anywhere from a few months to two years in length where you will learn about emergency medical procedures, human anatomy and physiology to become a qualified paramedic. You will then be awarded an official certification after passing written and practical examinations.

On top of certification, you may also need to obtain a paramedic license in order to practise professionally. The licensure process usually involves passing an exam pertaining to the requirements of the state or jurisdiction that you want to practise in before proceeding to fulfil a certain number of hours of continuing education after that. This is something to consider, especially if you choose to work as a paramedic overseas or in a different region from where you live.

Even after getting certified and licensed, much of your skills and learning as a paramedic will probably continue to be honed through real-life, on-the-job experiences. You may apply, or get posted by your training programme, to work as a paramedic for a hospital, fire department, or ambulance service.

And as you progress in your career over the years, you may also build up to higher appointments, taking on more responsibilities as Paramedic Overall-In-Charge or Emergency Medical Training Coordinator.

Do you feel excited to take on the undoubtedly demanding yet rewarding profession of a paramedic? Does saving lives as an emergency medical responder fill you with a sense of purpose and pride? And do you know you can begin your journey into the world of professional paramedicine right now? Yes, one way is to attend a junior first aid workshop that teaches you basic first aid knowledge.

These mini-courses teach you how to spot dangers in your environment, what to do during emergencies such as choking, poisoning, burns, and nosebleeds, and also which important numbers to call in times of need. The training is usually conducted by organisations such as the Red Cross or other civil defence groups that reach out to schools or operate in your local community.

C -
A -
B -

If you view a paramedic as a cross between an athlete - think speed and efficiency! - and a healthcare professional, then why not start by leading a fit and healthy lifestyle? You can also begin to cultivate your paramedical knowledge by learning about human anatomy, how our bodies function, and what are some of the best ways to restore someone back to optimal health after a sprained ankle or tummy ache.

If a healed human bone is indeed the first sign of civilisation, then paramedicine is surely the advancement of the care and support that we provide to fellow human beings beyond the hospital or clinic and in times of crisis, accidents, and disease.
Being a paramedic is not unlike being a modern-day warrior with equal measures of skill, compassion, and courage required to render the necessary life-saving procedures for all in need.

My Inspiration

Shubhi Saxena
Founder, Unibino

As a parent in this ever-changing world, it can sometimes feel overwhelming when it comes to our children's futures. New technologies seem to be arising almost every day, and with so many innovations, it creates unique professions which many of us wouldn't have dreamed to be necessary only a few years ago. Which to me is a good thing. Because with so much variety, my children can have the opportunity to pick a career that will fit their personalities and build upon their strengths. As you may imagine, this desire within me to provide my children with the resources they needed to thrive, led me to search out books that would be easy enough for them to understand while teaching them about various professions.

Only, I found that these books were few and far between. Even if I could find a book about a certain profession geared towards young readers, I found them sparse inside and limited to only certain careers that may not fit my children's abilities. This is when I came up with the idea to write my own children's books, teaching them about all the various careers in the modern world. After months of researching different professions and learning more than I ever expected, I quickly realised this was going to be a bigger project than I first anticipated. I dove into the histories of these professions, discovering links to the past, and why these professions were now so important.

Ultimately my goal was to offer my children options, to show them that there is no one set path for everyone. But in this, I stumbled upon something bigger. I wanted to share this with future generations. To share with all children and parents about these careers, to help spark curiosity, and to instil a passion for the future. Everyone has special talents and abilities, and I hope that this series will be able to offer clarity and inspiration to children around the world. Because at the end of the day, it's never too early to start dreaming and never too late to take action. With this, I hope you enjoy this series and that your young ones become the best versions of themselves as they can achieve.